From Acorns to Oak Trees

Written by Charles Cush
Illustrations by Adrian Williams

To Jean, my love and my partner for life; and to my children, for inspiring me.
—C.C.

To Shampree my Love; and my kids, for inspiring me to do what I do.
—A.W.

From Acorns to Oak Trees

Written by Charles Cush

Published by JoyLove Books
an imprint of Hadney Inc.
Fort Wayne, IN
Printed in USA
All rights reserved. No part of this book may be
reproduced, stored in a data retrieval system or
transmitted in any form by any means,
electronic, mechanical, photocopying,
recording or otherwise without the
permission of the copyright holder.
© 2008 Charles Cush

ISBN-10: 0-9818494-1-5
ISBN-13: 978-0-9818494-1-6

This is an acorn...

and this is me.

We do not look alike but share some similarities.

Like an acorn I am little now-- a tiny sight to see.
And like an acorn, there's potential locked up inside of me.

An acorn can grow up one day to be like this mighty oak tree.

But I can grow up to be ANYTHING I decide I want to be. Like...

a Doctor, a Lawyer, a Deep Sea Explorer,

or a Businessman who's always on the go.

A Chef,

a Librarian,

a Veterinarian,

or the Host of my own talk show.

An Actor,

a Writer,

a brave Firefighter,

or an Astronaut that flies into space.

A Musician,

a Preacher,

maybe even a Teacher,

or President of the United States!

To help it grow an acorn needs things, like

the sunshine and rain from above.

I need some things to help me too, like encouragement, and a whole lot of love.

My Mommy and Daddy teach me and they guide me as I grow.

Since I'm going to do great things someday, there's a lot I'll need to know.

They read to me and talk to me; they take me to the park and zoo.

Because it's important to feed my body, but my mind needs feeding, too!

Another thing they do, to help me on my way, is tell me they believe in me each and every day.

I know that if I try my best, there's nothing I can't do. And if you're a kid like I am, the same is true for you.

Anything is possible, just you wait and see.
Because like this acorn I'm little now...

but there's so much more I'll be!

About the Author

Charles Cush believes that every child has unlimited potential. He has a passion for helping others achieve their best in life; and wrote this book to remind his children (Marcus, Sydney, and Haley) that they can achieve anything they desire.

Charles lives in Fort Wayne, Indiana with his wife Jean, their children, and their dog Sparkles.

Adrian Williams is a talented designer and illustrator. He has been illustrating books since he was in the first grade, and is fulfilling his lifelong dream of being a successful artist.

Adrian lives in Fort Wayne, Indiana with his wife Shampree, and daughters Myka, Layla, and new baby boy Brooklyn.